M000034606

"The Old is Better"

SOME BIBLE VERSIONS CONSIDERED

By

ALFRED J. LEVELL

GOSPEL STANDARD TRUST PUBLICATIONS

1990

7 Brackendale Grove, Harpenden, Herts. AL5 3EL

ENGLAND

ISBN 0 903556 87 1

Printed in Great Britain
at Flair Press, Northampton

All scripture is given by inspiration of God, and is profitable for doctrine, for reproof, for correction, for instruction in righteousness: that the man of God may be perfect, throughly furnished unto all good works.

2 Timothy 3. 16, 17

No prophecy of the scripture is of any private interpretation. For the prophecy came not in old time by the will of man: but holy men of God spake as they were moved by the Holy Ghost.

2 Peter 1. 20, 21

David...said, The spirit of the LORD spake by me, and his word was in my tongue.

2 Samuel 23. 1, 2

The words of the LORD are pure words: as silver tried in a furnace of earth, purified seven times.

Psalm 12. 6

Thy word is very pure: therefore thy servant loveth it.

Psalm 119. 140

Every word of God is pure.   Proverbs 30. 5

For ever, O LORD, thy word is settled in heaven.   Psalm 119. 89

The Lord gave the word: great was the company of those that published it.

Psalm 68. 11

For whatsoever things were written aforetime were written for our learning, that we through patience and comfort of the scriptures might have hope.

Romans 15. 4

For I testify unto every man that heareth the words of the prophecy of this book, If any man shall add unto these things, God shall add unto him the plagues that are written in this book. And if any man shall take away from the words of the book of this prophecy, God shall take away his part out of the book of life, and out of the holy city, and from the things which are written in this book.

Revelation 22. 18, 19

Thou hast magnified thy word above all thy name.   Psalm 138. 2

iii

CONTENTS

CHAPTER 1

INTRODUCTION

Why have I written this booklet? Because I have had a burden on my spirit for young people in their late teens and early twenties who are concerned about the things of God and who are faced with the problem of so many versions of the English Bible in these days. They may have been brought up on the Authorised Version, and wonder whether they should stick to that or not. Or they may have gone over to some other version in earlier life and now wonder whether others are keeping to the Authorised Version simply because they are old fashioned or because there is some real reason for doing so. It is a problem that those of us who are older never had in our younger days because for all practical purposes there was only one English Bible, THE Bible; the Authorised Version.There might be differences of interpretation — and there were — but there was not in general any dispute about the words of this version; and many were attracted anyway by its beautiful language and its reverent style. It was the Bible in use in our churches and in our schools.

But now all is changed. Many evangelical Christians have switched to the Revised Standard Version (RSV) or to the New International Version (NIV) or, more recently, to the New King James Version (NKJV). What is the average young man or woman to make of all this? There are many scholarly books on these matters, and the more one reads such books the more one realises what a complex field of study is the study of manuscripts and printed editions of the Hebrew and Greek texts. This booklet is an attempt, from a conservative point of view, to give an outline of the subject in plain words. It is not intended to be a scholarly work or an exhaustive

1

study, but to give serious enquirers some guidance on possible further reading — hence a Bibliography is included at Appendix A — and to help those who do not have the time or the mind for further reading to get a basic understanding of how we got our Bible, and why the Authorised Version (AV) may still be regarded as the best available English translation of the Holy Scriptures, in spite of all the criticisms and developments this century.

The writer, in serving on the Committee of the Trinitarian Bible Society (TBS) for some years, and as its Chairman for nearly 11 years, has had the opportunity and the incentive to read a number of the scholarly works about the Hebrew and Greek texts of the Scriptures and about the technical aspects of Bible translation work. In writing this booklet, he seeks to distil something of this reading, in layman's terms, for the benefit of others. At the same time, he emphasises that the views expressed in the following chapters are his own, and are not necessarily those of the Trinitarian Bible Society, although it would not be surprising if there is a fairly large area of agreement.

The author's thanks are given to the following gentlemen who read the draft of this booklet and gave helpful criticism and suggestions: The Rev. B. G. Felce M.A., Messrs. A. J. Barker M.A., C.Eng., F.I.E.E., H. J. W. Legerton F.C.A., T.P. Letis B.A., M.T.S., B. A. Ramsbottom B.A., T. J. Ramsbottom B.A., and D. P. Rowland; and also to two friends in Bedfordshire who kindly typed the manuscript and made the subsequent alterations in it. Grateful acknowledgment is also made of quotations of and from various TBS publications.

CHAPTER 2

THE BACKGROUND OF CHANGE

God's people in every age, more or less, since the time of Jesus Christ have believed that they were living in the last times. But things have gone on, and on; and from this unbelievers argue, as Peter said they would (2 Peter 3. 3-14), against the second coming of our Lord and the end of the world. Or else they are just unconcerned about such things. But there are features of life in the second half of the 20th century that point to a great difference from earlier ages and show more clearly than ever before that we are now in the last days. One particular feature is the extraordinary and ever-increasing pace of change in the last 150 years. To make clear what I have in mind, suppose someone in the time of Abraham could have revisited the earth 2000 years later in the 1st century A.D. He would have found life much as he had known it — oxen still drawing the plough, horses and carts going along dusty tracks, buildings much the same though no doubt technically improved. Similarly if someone from the 1st century in the time of the Apostle John could have seen life 1000 years later, in the 11th century, the same general picture would have emerged. No doubt there would have been further improvements in some ways, but life would have been much as he had known it. Again if someone from the 11th century in the time of William the Conqueror could have seen life in the 18th century when the Wesleys and George Whitefield were alive, the ships would have been better, but still driven by wind-power; the carts and coaches would have been better, but still drawn by horses. Bows and arrows would have been replaced by guns, and printed books would have been in existence over 200 years. But for the most part life was not fundamentally different in the

18th century from the 11th. But now, jumping from the 18th century to the 20th — a mere 200 years — what a vast change! Notably the developments in transport, communications, medicine, industry, house-building and so on, together with the explosion in population, have brought about a complete transformation, and life in the late 20th century is greatly different from life before, say, 1800. This ever-increasing rate of change, taken with the vast increase in world population in the last two centuries, and the widespread scale of wickedness and godlessness, as foreshadowed in such scriptures as 2 Timothy 3 and 2 Peter 3, are pointers indeed to the last days. Daniel 12. 4 is also relevant.

But just looking at, say, the last 50 years, in that short time there have been some remarkable developments, and some of these are listed below.

1. The massive spread of car ownership and road transport generally, and therefore motorways and great urban traffic and environment problems.
2. Air travel, and space travel, even to putting men on the moon.
3. Splitting the atom; nuclear power; and the nuclear threat.
4. The computer revolution.
5. Radio and telephone communications, world-wide, including satellites.
6. Television and videos, their rapid spread, and the resultant effects on life-style and behaviour.
7. The many English versions of the Holy Scriptures that have been published, at a time when English has become the world's leading language.

These things, and others not mentioned, have had marked effects, and reveal the ever-quickening pace of change, and the fact that we are all living in a very different world from that of our predecessors. One result of some of the developments listed is that our age has become very materialistic, much taken up with entertainment and sport, for which television provides unprecedented facilities — and God is largely forgotten, or ignored. So the general picture is very much like what the Holy Scriptures have to say about the last times, especially in the passages already referred to. God alone knows the time of the end, but we need wisdom to see and ponder the signs of the times.

Against this background, and the marked decline in real religion in this century in our own land, the last change mentioned earlier — the multiplying of English versions of the Bible — is remarkable. There has not been a time like it since the canon of Scripture was given and formed in the first century A.D. Why has this come about? One reason has been that in the period from about 1850 to 1950, there was much study by scholars of the manuscripts and texts of the Scriptures, and regrettably a departure in some respects from the traditional underlying texts of Scripture. No doubt there was also a sincere desire to produce English versions in more modern English; but some were spoilt by too colloquial a style of English. Furthermore, one cannot ignore the fact that money and the profit motive have played some part. But what has been the effect of all these versions? Is the world, or our own country, any better? Is Christianity any deeper or more extensive? Is reverence for God and acknowledgment of His Name any greater? Alas! No! One clear result has been the spreading of confusion among the churches, and in this one detects, underlying everything else, the work of that arch-enemy of God's people, the devil himself. Satan has always been the enemy of God's Word, both the incarnate Word, Jesus Christ Himself, and the written

Word. Looking back over the centuries, how much persecution has he been instrumental in bringing upon those who have been faithful to God's Word, and have prized it above all earthly possessions. There has been much bitter enmity against the Scriptures, with burnings of Bibles, confiscation and similar measures. But God has wonderfully preserved His Word from all its external enemies down through the ages.

In these days of religious toleration, it would seem that Satan has changed his tactics, and is attacking the Church of God more from within, by causing doubts to be cast on the traditional text, by bringing about a multiplication of new English translations, and thus sowing confusion and argument among the churches. "God is not the author of confusion, but of peace" (1 Corinthians 14. 33). These new versions cause disunity; they tend generally, especially those whose language is more akin to that of a newspaper, to reduce reverence for Almighty God; and they are destroying much of the memorisation of Scripture, especially by children and young people, which has been such a blessing in the past. On the other hand, it must be acknowledged that, in spite of their faults, God has doubtless used them in the conversion or instruction of some. He is a Sovereign in what means He uses, or if He chooses to use none. The fact remains that most of these versions are unsound, and they have turned many aside from a sound version. They sow doubt upon certain passages of God's Word, by omissions or alterations, and also by misleading footnotes about the text or about the reliability of the underlying manuscripts. Was it not the devil who asked the first question in the Bible: "Yea, hath God said?" It was the devil's work then to cast doubts on the truth and the words of Almighty God, and it still is. Christ Himself said of the devil, "He is a liar and the father of it" (John 8. 44).

CHAPTER 3

THE MAIN ENGLISH VERSIONS

In this chapter we will very briefly consider the main English versions of the Bible from the Authorised Version onwards. Many versions are now available — probably more than a hundred of the New Testament — but we will only mention the most important and widely-used ones.

The Authorised Version, 1611 (AV)

The decision to proceed with a new translation of the Holy Scriptures was taken at the Hampton Court Conference of 1604, (chaired by King James I), and to accomplish this task some fifty-four translators were appointed. They were all eminent scholars, and they all had great reverence for the Word of God, being wholly committed to its inspiration and infallibility. They were drawn from a wide spectrum, from what would be known as ''High Church'' to the Puritan element in the Church of England. They organised themselves into six groups — two at Westminster, one for the Old Testament and one for the New; two at Oxford, one for each Testament; and two at Cambridge, one for the Old Testament, and one for the Apocrypha. When, after much careful labour, the draft translations were ready, editing and revision work were undertaken by six of the translators (two each from the Oxford, Cambridge and London groups), who worked daily for nine months at Stationers Hall, London. Then a final editing and revision was carried out by Bishop Bilson of Winchester (from the Cambridge group), who had High Church views, and Doctor Miles Smith (from the Oxford group), who had Puritan leanings. Doctor Miles Smith also wrote the eloquent and lengthy preface to the translation — not to be confused with the dedicatory preface to King James I

— and in this translators' preface the humility of the writer and of the translators is to be remarked. Here also the principles followed by the translators are to be found.

The translators drew on the earlier 16th century translations, such as the Bishops' Bible and the Geneva Bible, but especially on Tyndale's translation. His was a very great influence on the Authorised Version — it has been said that some 80% or more of the AV derives from Tyndale. In a sense the AV was the culmination of nearly a century of Bible translation; it reaped from what had gone before, as well as from the eminent scholarship and reverent godliness of the chosen translators; it came out of the Reformation which was the greatest revival since the first Christian Pentecost. For some years after its publication in 1611, the AV did not meet with universal approval, but in course of time, its truth, and the beautiful, rhythmic English in which it was expressed, found a lasting place in the hearts of the British people; so that the historian J. R. Green could say that "England became the people of a book, and that book was the Bible." What is not so generally known is that in the 1760s, two scholars (Dr. Thomas Paris of Cambridge and Dr. Benjamin Blayney of Oxford) gave the book an orthographical revision i.e. a revision confined to spelling and punctuation. This was a most necessary thing, and if it had not been done we should hardly have been able to read the AV today. Something more could still be done in this direction since some spellings are now obsolete, for example, musick for music, publick for public, sodering for soldering, subtil for subtle.

The Revised Version, New Testament 1881, Old Testament 1885 (RV)

In the latter half of the 19th century a movement was started whose aim was to have the Authorised Version revised.

Originally it seems that a conservative revision was in mind — orthography, archaic words etc. — but as time went on, the revision project appears to have been "hi-jacked" by Professor Westcott and Dr. Hort (of whom, more later) so that it became a much more radical revision, with the New Testament being based on a different Greek text, compiled by Westcott and Hort and considered by them to be a great improvement, but considered by some conservative Biblical scholars to be much less reliable than that which underlies the AV. (See chapter 4). The Revised Version (New Testament) appeared in 1881, and initially met with some success, but this died down and the complete Bible, published in 1885, never found much favour. It was regarded with suspicion and disapproval by many, and it never achieved anything like the acceptance and popularity of the AV. Now, a hundred years later, the AV is still loved and respected wherever the English language is spoken, while the RV is scarcely heard of.

Note. All the following versions, with one exception (which will be indicated), are based on a similar type of New Testament text to that of the Revised Version, and thus all these versions are flawed in the same basic way.

American Standard Version, 1901 (ASV)

This is the American Version of the Revised Version, with a more thorough elimination of older words, and of words that are specifically English rather than American.

Revised Standard Version, New Testament 1946, Bible 1952 (RSV)

This was prepared by a Committee representing 40 Protestant denominations in the USA and Canada. It is in modern speech, but professes to use *"Thou"* when referring to God, and *"you"* when referring to man. However, sadly, the disciples are made to say *"You"* in speaking to Christ e.g. Matthew 16. 16, "You are the Christ, the Son of the living God." Yet He is equal with God the Father in power and glory. One feature of this and other modern versions is that they do not make the clear acknowledgment of Christ's deity that is found in the AV. The RSV was revised in 1972, and has just been revised again in 1990. *"Thou"* and *"Thee"* were eliminated in 1972.

The New English Bible, New Testament 1961, Bible 1970 (NEB)

This was prepared by a Committee representing nine denominations in Great Britain. This, again, is in modern speech, sometimes descending to the colloquial, and it has the same convention of using *"Thou"* when referring to God and *"you"* when referring to man. But, as with the RSV, *"you"* is used in speaking to Christ. Also the word "worship," while being applied to God is, with one exception, not applied to Christ, the alternatives used being "paying homage" or "bowing." What a loss this is, for example, in John 9. 38, as well as an insult to the eternal Son of God!

New American Standard Version 1960 (NASV)

This is a revision, as its name implies, of the ASV. While it is more accurate than some other modern versions, it suffers from the weakness of its underlying text, and clouds the testimony of the Holy Scriptures to the person and glory of the eternal Son of God.

Today's English Version, New Testament 1966, Bible 1976 (TEV)

This is also known as "Good News for Modern Man" (GNB), and was published by the American Bible Society. It suffers from similar weakness in its underlying text, and in addition the translator in many passages which mention the "blood" of Jesus has substituted the word "death," contrary to the evidence of the manuscripts. This version has therefore sometimes been called "the bloodless Bible." It is also profusely illustrated by line drawings, or cartoons, many of which are inappropriate or unnecessary in a book such as the Holy Bible. The style of English is modern and readable, but the translation is broad and suffers much from the use of "dynamic equivalence" (see Chapter 5).

The Jerusalem Bible 1966

This is a Roman Catholic version, but was authorised for use in the Church of England in 1969 — the first time since the Reformation that a Roman Catholic translation has been so authorised. The full version contains many notes and in these Roman Catholic teaching (e.g. on the Mass), as well as modernistic thought, is very evident. This Bible was originally published in French in 1955, having been prepared by French Roman Catholic scholars at L'Ecole Biblique (The Biblical School) in Jerusalem: that appears to be the rather tenuous reason why the modern English translation was called "The Jerusalem Bible." This version was revised in 1985 and is now called **"The New Jerusalem Bible."**

The Living Bible 1971

This version is really more a paraphrase than a translation; many of its renderings are arbitrary, and the style of English, while it may be modern, leaves much to be desired, including as it sometimes does colloquial and even slang phrases and words. It is an unreliable version both in its content and in its expression.

New International Version, New Testament 1973, Bible 1978 (NIV)

This version was published by the New York Bible Society (now known as the International Bible Society). Apart from the unsatisfactory text on which it is based, the English style of the translation is better than that of some other modern versions, such as the NEB, but is not without its shortcomings and a considerable amount of paraphrasing. Dr. R. P. Martin in his excellent critique of the NIV (see Bibliography) expresses his conclusion thus (page 70): "The NIV is not worthy of becoming the standard version of the English-speaking world. Its accuracy is suspect in too many ways." In addition, the use of *"Thou"* and *"Thee"* is completely eliminated, and many will regret this. (This question is dealt with in chapter 6.) The NIV has been widely accepted among evangelical believers in this country in spite of the unsatisfactory character of its underlying text and of its translation method.

The New King James Version, New Testament 1979, Bible 1982 (NKJV)

This modern version is a refreshing change because the New Testament is based on virtually the same Greek text as the AV, although the Old Testament is based on a somewhat different Hebrew text from the AV. In this respect it stands alone among the modern versions. It was produced in America and was the product of the combined labours of a team of "130 of the world's most respected theologians, scholars and editors." It has a generally good style of

English, but, in the view of some of us, this is marred by the elimination of the pronouns *"Thou"* and *"Thee,"* and by other blemishes of detail. This version is given more detailed consideration in chapter 7.

The Revised English Bible, 1989 (REB)

This is a revision of the NEB, and virtually replaces it — which goes to show that some of these modern versions will have a comparatively short life-span, and it is doubtful whether any will achieve the lasting acceptability which has been such a characteristic of the AV. The REB was produced by a ''Joint Committee'' on which there were official representatives of the Roman Catholic Church. It remedies some of the defects of the NEB, but still leaves others; it eliminates the pronouns *"Thou"* and *"Thee."* But, above all, it remains on the same unsatisfactory textual basis as the NEB.

Lastly, perhaps mention should be made, by way of warning, of *The New World Translation,* which is the main Jehovah's Witnesses' Bible. It was published in portions during the 1950s, and the complete Bible came out in 1961, the New Testament being based on the Westcott and Hort type of Greek text. The sect also publish ''The Bible in Living English'' (not to be confused with the Living Bible); an edition of the AV, with marginal references; and an ''Interlinear translation of the Greek Scriptures,'' which is a word-for-word translation of the Westcott and Hort text. Thus there arise many inconsistencies between the Bibles used by the sect, but their Bibles have one common characteristic, that they have a Unitarian bias. Jehovah's Witnesses do not believe in the deity of the Lord Jesus Christ, and the Westcott and Hort Greek text, together with their own renderings in translation, help them to obscure, or omit altogether, passages of Scripture that bear testimony to this cardinal doctrine of our Christian faith.

To sum up, all this proliferation of versions of the Bible in the last 40 years has sown confusion among the churches in our land, and in the English-speaking world. It has not brought about a real revival of religion. In fact the period of their publication has coincided with a period of great spiritual and moral decline. The translations that bring the Bible down to the level of man tend to weaken respect and reverence for the Holy Scriptures.

In assessing the merits or demerits of any translation of the Holy Scriptures we need to ask two basic questions:

1. On what Hebrew and Greek manuscripts or text has the translation been based? This is fundamental, because no translation — not even the very best — can be satisfactory if it has translated something that is unsatisfactory in itself.

2. How accurate, faithful, fitting and well-expressed is the translation?

These two themes will be taken up in the next two chapters.

CHAPTER 4

THE HEBREW AND GREEK TEXTS

Until the invention of printing in the 15th century, all copies of the Holy Scriptures were *manuscripts* i.e. written by hand. All books or manuscripts wear out or get lost or damaged in the course of centuries, and so copies had to be made. Copies were obviously needed also for the spreading of God's truth. But the copying process is itself likely to produce errors: we all know how easy it is to make a mistake in copying something out, particularly if it is old and difficult to read. The study of all the manuscripts now in existence with a view to defining the true text, and eliminating errors, is called "textual criticism." The late Dr. E. F. Hills of USA has said that "Textual criticism endeavours to discover and repair the damage incurred (by manuscripts) during the voyage over the sea of time."

Here I would like to emphasise the enormous complexity, and the wide field, of this subject, and say at once that I can only touch the fringe of it. It can be, and has been for some scholars, a lifetime's study. There is much opportunity for divergence of view. Some scholars would treat the Bible as just another ancient book, whose text they can study by all the usual methods of textual criticism. But this is where they go wrong: it is not the right approach for the Holy Scriptures, which are a unique book. The right approach here is a *believing* approach; that is, *believing* that God Himself inspired the very words of Scripture, as given originally, as is stated in various places in the Bible, notably:

2 Timothy 3. 16. "All Scripture is given by inspiration of God, and is profitable...." (This is mis-translated in many modern versions to make it appear that some Scriptures are

inspired and some not: the AV gives the correct translation.)

2 Peter 1. 21. "... holy men of God spake as they were moved by the Holy Ghost."

2 Samuel 23. 2. (among David's last words) "The Spirit of the Lord spake by me, and his word was in my tongue."

It is not the function of this booklet to go into the doctrine of "Inspiration," but it is one of the foundation stones of true Christian faith. It is also a mystery as to how it was done, but it does appear that God used the individual abilities and writing styles of the men He chose for this work, and they were not mere automatons or "dictating machines." They wrote what God had breathed into their minds and hearts, and the result was the only piece of infallible writing the world has ever seen, in which God has given a most precious revelation of Himself, and of the Lord Jesus Christ His eternal Son. Those who study the ancient manuscripts, (and those who translate), need always to bear in mind the special character of the book. It is not just another work of man: it is the divinely-inspired Word of God.

Basically, the original Scriptures were written in Hebrew for the Old Testament, and in Greek for the New Testament. But, of course, we no longer have the "original autographs" - the manuscripts written by the inspired prophets and other writers. All we have are *copies* of these manuscripts. What scholars have done in the past and what textual critics still seek to do is to collate and compare the manuscripts in detail, passage by passage, and sometimes word by word. If the scholar is working on the principle that the majority of the readings for any particular passage will give the true reading for that passage, then the detailed readings that have the greatest numerical support among the manuscripts are incorporated into a printed text, and the variant readings may be given in an organised structure of footnotes, which is called a ''critical apparatus.'' (If, however, the scholar were following the Westcott and Hort principle that the most ancient manuscripts are the most reliable, then he would incorporate in the text the readings from those manuscripts which he judged to be the oldest and best and would show other readings as variants in the footnotes.) By this kind of technique printed texts are derived from the manuscripts and, while the techniques may have become more sophisticated, it was primarily this basic method (using the principle of the numerical majority of readings) which gave us the 16th and 17th Century printed editions of the New Testament which became known as the Textus Receptus.

For the Old Testament, the copying of manuscripts was done with extreme care by the Jewish priesthood in the centuries before Christ. The Apostle Paul, speaking of the advantages of the Jews, says, ''Much every way: chiefly, because that unto them were committed the oracles of God'' (Romans 3. 2). After the time of Christ, copies were made by Jewish scribes, and especially by those from the 6th century onwards called the Masoretes, who took extraordinary pains to ensure the correctness of their copies. Thus God used the meticulous copying by the Jewish priests and scribes to preserve the Old Testament portion of His inspired Word. At the end of the mediaeval period, it was this traditional (Masoretic) text that was used for the first printed Hebrew Bible in 1488.

There was also a translation of the Old Testament into Greek before the time of Christ, called the Septuagint because it was done by 70 scholars. The apostles of the Lord Jesus sometimes quoted in the New Testament from this translation and sometimes from the Hebrew Scriptures. The translation, which was not without some faults, was widely accepted and used in the early Christian church.

Turning now to the New Testament, the position is very different, and there seems to be much more controversy about the New Testament manuscripts than there is about the Old Testament ones. At present, there have been discovered just over 5000 manuscripts containing parts of varying size of the New Testament — many are indeed only small parts. These are held in museums, colleges, churches, etc., throughout the western world. In brief, there are three "families" of the NT manuscripts: the Byzantine (or "Traditional") emanating from the Asia Minor/ Constantinople (Istanbul)/Greece area (where, of course, Paul founded a number of churches); the Western family centred on Rome; and the Alexandrian family centred on Alexandria in Egypt. The Byzantine family is by far the most numerous, and also these manuscripts have a very large measure of agreement between themselves. They are the ones that have historically been followed by the Church, and the "Traditional Text" derives from them. Eventually, certain 16th and 17th century printed editions of this text became known as the "Textus Receptus," or "Received Text," and this is the text which, with just a few minor exceptions, underlies our Authorised Version. This traditional text is supported by the vast majority of all extant manuscripts, and the conservative view has been that the majority of the manuscripts, with but a few small exceptions, can be relied on to give the true text of the Scriptures.* Very plainly, over the years, the blessing of God has rested conspicuously on good translations (like the AV, and Luther's German Bible) of this text.

---

* but see the last paragraph of this chapter (pages 22, 23)

But about 150 years ago some older manuscripts came to light, and certain textual critics under the leadership and example of two scholars named Professor Westcott and Dr. Hort, took the view that these older manuscripts should be given much greater weight in assessing what was the true text, even though these manuscripts were far fewer, and also did not agree among themselves. They were mainly of the Alexandrian family, and were notable for having many shorter readings than the traditional text. However, the criterion of the age of the manuscripts — as distinct from numbers and mutual agreement — prevailed among the 19th century scholars, although there were some who raised their voices against it. So all the versions of the Scriptures, from the Revised Version of 1881 onwards, have been based mainly on these older Alexandrian manuscripts. This modern text is defended on the grounds that the older, earlier manuscripts are to be preferred in spite of manifest shortcomings in them, and the fact that there are serious differences between themselves. Use of these manuscripts has been the fashionable thing in Biblical textual scholarship for the last 100 years. (Compare the situation on the teaching of evolution in our schools as fact instead of theory!) Those scholars who support the traditional text — and they have been growing somewhat in recent years — believe that these manuscripts were older, *unreliable* copies, and the Church of God, centuries ago, under the guiding hand of God, abandoned them as faulty and unsound, but continued to copy out manuscripts of the traditional text, which wore out more frequently, simply because they were more used. One of the most famous of the older manuscripts, but in the view of many conservative scholars very unreliable, is the Codex Sinaiticus, discovered in a monastery on Sinai in 1859, and dating from the 4th century AD. (It is now in the British Library.) This

19

manuscript and Codex Vaticanus (held by the Vatican), are given great weight by the scholars who follow Westcott and Hort, as being very ancient (both date from the 4th century), and therefore more to be relied on. But these two manuscripts differ from each other more than 3000 times in the Gospels alone! (See article in TBS Quarterly Record No. 510 of January 1990.)

The other family of manuscripts not yet dealt with is the Western one. These Western manuscripts tend to incorporate here and there longer readings than the Traditional text. They have been mainly used for Roman Catholic Bibles, notably the Latin Vulgate of the 4th century, and the Douay Version of 1582.

One needs to be a scholar, with a good knowledge of Greek, to follow all the detailed arguments about the relationship of these three families of manuscripts, but in the writer's view, the balance of argument is strongly in favour of the traditional text. But there is another, and very important point. God has wonderfully preserved His Word. He promised in Isaiah 40. 8., that "the Word of our God shall stand for ever," and this was confirmed by the Apostle Peter in 1 Peter 1. 25. He preserved His Word by various means. He used first of all the meticulous care of the priests and scribes in copying the manuscripts. In the Christian era His Church was to be the custodian of His Holy Word, and the Traditional text (as it has become known) was the one preserved and used by the Church for many centuries. His providence has ensured that something like 80%-90% of the preserved manuscripts are of the Byzantine family, and that there is a very large measure of agreement indeed between them. As already remarked, His blessing has rested in a very marked degree on translations made from the Traditional Text. Moreover, seeing that God inspired "Holy men of

God'' to write the various books constituting His Word, is it not unthinkable that He would have left the world without a true version of His Word for over 1800 years? To ask the question is to supply the answer! He has wonderfully inspired His Word, and He has wonderfully preserved it. We can be sure that when we hold our AV Bibles in our hand, we hold the true Word of God in all material respects.

Before leaving the subject of the underlying manuscripts, a comment is called for on the fact that because all modern versions (except the NKJV) are based on a Westcott and Hort type of text, derived mainly from the Alexandrian family of manuscripts, there are many serious omissions in the New Testament. The largest omission is the last 12 verses of Mark, and neither the external evidence nor the internal evidence supports this omission: well over 90% of the evidence is the other way. Another omission is the account of the woman taken in adultery in John 8. 1-11. Then there are lots of individual verses, sentences, phrases and words omitted. Dr. J. A. Moorman has estimated that if all these omitted portions in the NIV, for example, are totalled up, the total is about equivalent to the total words in the two Epistles of Peter. Imagine the New Testament cut short like this! But what must God think of this in the light of His threatened judgment against this very thing in Revelation 22. 19? For this reason alone, it is well to leave such versions alone. It has been sad to see how the NIV has been so widely taken up in Evangelical and some Strict Baptist circles, who have forsaken the sound AV in favour of this less sound version.

One of the best and most readable summaries of these matters concerning the underlying texts of the New Testament is an article by an eminent American lawyer, Philip Mauro, who lived in the early part of this century. This article, entitled ''Which Version? Authorised or Revised?,'' is reproduced at pages 56-122 of "True or False?" edited by Dr. D. O. Fuller (see Bibliography) and is a critique of the Revised Version of 1881/85. In pages 56-90 the author deals well with the authenticity, or otherwise, of the various Greek manuscripts and explains the various faults and weaknesses of the modern Greek New Testament texts which rely on a few older manuscripts.

Another facet of the New Testament problem is mentioned by Professor Jakob van Bruggen at page 124 in his book "The Future of the Bible." He makes the following very pertinent comment about the growing uncertainty since 1881 of critics in regard to the New Testament text: "Critics today no longer choose one manuscript or textual group as the basic text, but reconstruct from all sorts of manuscripts a new hypothetical text. The Greek New Testament of the UBS (United Bible Societies), for example, is based upon the majority vote of five textual scholars, but not on the majority of 90% of the manuscripts. The result is that the textual basis for modern translations is subject to fluctuation."

Finally, mention should be made of what has come to be known as the "Majority Text," in regard to the New Testament. Certain scholars in our own day believe that the true original text lies in the majority readings of the Greek manuscripts, and such a text has been printed and published in America by the publishers of the NKJV (Thomas Nelson) and is called the Hodges/Farstad text after its editors Prof. Hodges and Dr. Farstad. But the reader will ask: "Have you not said that the AV New Testament is based on the majority of Greek manuscripts?" Yes, that is indeed so, but the rule of the majority of Greek manuscripts was not applied so rigidly and inflexibly, as these modern scholars would do. Regard was had by the editors of the Textus Receptus and by the AV translators, here and there, as the occasion seemed to demand, to Latin manuscripts (of which there are many) and to other sources considered by them to be sound, such as the quotations of Scripture made by many of the early fathers. In this the writer believes that these men and scholars like Theodore Beza (1519-1605) — who prepared several editions of the Greek New Testament text — were guided by God, so that His Word has been faithfully preserved. Perhaps the most important instance concerns 1 John 5. 7, 8, where there is very little Greek manuscript support for most of these two verses, but there is some support in Latin sources. The matter has been argued over for centuries, but whereas the AV translators accepted the inclusion of the disputed passage (called the ''Johannine Comma'') in the ''Textus Receptus'' - to which it had been imported from the Latin — those who take a strictly ''Majority Text'' position would exclude it. The differences between the Greek text underlying the AV and this Majority Text are nothing like as numerous or as weighty as the differences between the AV text and the Nestlé/United Bible Societies text which follows Westcott and Hort principles and is (with variations) the text underlying most modern versions. Nevertheless, the implication of this modern ''Majority Text'' position is that we have not yet quite got to the original true text inspired by God, and we must go on studying to find it. The writer believes that God, having inspired His Word, has ensured its preservation, in all material respects, as we have it in the Greek text underlying the AV. God would not have left us for nearly 2000 years without the true text of His Word, and even then to be still uncertainly trying to find it!

CHAPTER 5

THOUGHTS ON TRANSLATIONS

Our second point mentioned at the end of chapter 3 was the accuracy and faithfulness of a translation and how fitting and well-expressed it is. There is such a tendency in modern versions of the Bible to give priority to readability, at some expense in either accuracy, or dignity, or reverence — or all three!

In the first place a would-be translator of the Holy Scriptures should remember that it is the words inspired by God that he has to translate. He does not have the same degree of freedom as someone translating a secular work. Yet, of course, all of us who have studied languages, and have had translating work to do, realise that you cannot just translate word for word. Languages differ in their construction, in their range of words and in their idiom. The translator has to take account of these features in the "receptor" language, and act accordingly to the best of his ability. The translator should recognise regular features both of grammar and of idiom in both the language from which the translation is being made, and in the "receptor" language, but, in the case of the Scriptures, try to keep as close to the literal words as he possibly can.

Another point is that a translator of the Bible should refrain from incorporating comment or explanation in his translation. Some of the modern translations do not succeed in doing this always. It is the task of the translator to translate and give the actual meaning of the original words, leaving it to the preacher (or commentator) to explain the meaning and possible implications of the text. An example of the breaking of this rule is given in respect of Luke 1. 10 in TBS Leaflet 19A on the NIV, as follows:

24

Luke 1. 10 "all the assembled worshippers" (AV "the whole multitude of the people"). Here the NIV introduces two ideas which are not in the original Greek. There is no word here in the Greek meaning either "assembled" or "worshippers." It can be deduced from the context that the people had indeed assembled together, and that their purpose was to worship, but this is not the primary meaning of the Greek. The NIV fails to distinguish translation from explanation. It is the task of the preacher or commentator to explain the implications of the text, but the task of the translator is to give the actual meaning of the original words.

This leads on to some modern thought on translation of the Scriptures. In recent times, a new principle of translation has come to the fore, called *"Dynamic Equivalence."* The main advocate of this has been a scholar by the name of Eugene Nida. Under this theory, one translates the idea rather than the actual words, so that the impact of the translation on the reader is much the same as the impact of the original words on the original reader. In one sense this may be a quite laudable objective but it gives scope for the exercise of considerable subjective judgment. Obviously, where necessary, our AV translators paid attention to the idea and spirit of a passage where the languages differed in structure, and it was difficult to translate absolutely literally, word for word. But our AV translators were sound and scholarly men, who had a profound regard for the very words of God, and aimed at a full translation of the words, that is, *"complete equivalence."* In general, the AV is based on this approach. To explain what is meant by "dynamic equivalence," and taking a rather extreme example to illustrate the pitfalls: supposing a translation of Isaiah is being done for an equatorial tribe or nation, who have never seen snow. It would be better according to the advocates of dynamic equivalence to translate Isaiah 1. 18, ''Though your sins be as scarlet they shall be as white as snow'' by saying ''as white as cornflour,'' which is something the tribe knows about. But then what happens when the translators come to Isaiah 55. 10 ''For as the rain descendeth and the snow from heaven''? You can hardly translate that as ''cornflour''! The case shows the difference between the clever natural mind and the believing spiritual mind. The believing translator will reverence the doctrine of divine inspiration of the words, and he will say ''God has said 'snow': it is my duty to translate the words God has inspired,'' and he will leave teachers and others to explain what snow is e.g. by means of pictures and photos. It is the job of the Bible translator to translate what God has said, and not what *he* thinks may be better or clearer. Ministers have their part to play in explaining and interpreting the Word of God. The translation does, of course, need to be in good English, and as clear as possible; but we all need ever to remember that God alone, by His Spirit, can reveal the truth, ''The natural man receiveth not the things of the Spirit of God'' (1 Corinthians 2. 14). Some modern versions have come down to a very colloquial standard. Others, especially where dynamic equivalence has been used to any extent, are really paraphrases rather than translations.

Lastly, the language of a translation of the Scriptures needs to be fitting and reverent. The language of the newspaper is not appropriate, and, however ''readable'' it may be, it will not forward the work of God at all. Colloquial expressions are often comparatively short-lived. Those of us who are older can look back to phrases in use in our young days, but now no longer heard; and today's catch phrases will probably disappear just as quickly. The use of common

26

contractions such as "Don't," "Won't," etc., is also to be avoided. However people may criticise the "ancient language" of the AV, it is good English, and basically much of it is very simple, with a high proportion of words of one syllable. Read John 10, for example, with this point in mind. From the literary point of view the AV with its beautiful rhythm and cadences, is surely the jewel in the crown of the priceless literary heritage of the English language. Let us not neglect it, or throw it away.

CHAPTER 6

"THOU" or "YOU"?

This is a difficult matter, but "the nettle must be grasped"!

The second person singular pronouns, *"Thou"* and *"Thee," "Thy," "Thine,"* with the accompanying verb ending "est," and the verb ending "eth" for the third person, are now all regarded by many as archaic, and therefore not to be used in any modern translation of the Bible. There is a good case for dropping "eth" e.g. Psalm 103. 14 "For he knoweth our frame; he remembereth that we are dust" would become "For he knows our frame; he remembers that we are dust." There is no loss of accuracy or reverence here, but there is simply the loss of the dignity and rhythm of the AV. However, for the second person pronouns, the position is different, because the change does lead to a loss of accuracy of translation and also to a loss of reverence.

Taking the matter of reverence first, the reader will be aware that in many religious circles, including many Evangelicals, *"You"* and *"Your"* have been widely adopted in prayer to God instead of *"Thou," "Thee," "Thy," "Thine."* It seems to be the "in thing" in those circles, and they will argue that it does not betoken a lack of reverence. Reverence, they will say, is the attitude of the heart, and *"You"* and *"Your"* can be just as reverently intended as *"Thou"* and *"Thee."* While we know that reverence *must* be in the heart, the outward way in which that reverence is expressed cannot be dismissed so lightly. I believe this modern trend is all part of the general lack of respect for authority and of the tendency these days to bring God down to our human level. But what does Scripture say? In Psalm 50 part of verse 21 God says, "Thou thoughtest that I was altogether such an one as thyself: but I will reprove thee."

28

Speaking personally, this has been a voice to me in the matter, and I believe that the *"You"* and *"Your"* habit does in time lead to an undue familiarity and a loss of reverence.

A further point is that the use of *"Thou"* and *"Thee,"* etc., in prayer to God has been a feature of the English language for many centuries — ten at least — irrespective of what the normal secular practice has been. Even in 1881 — only just over 100 years ago — when the Revised Version was published, and when *"You"* had become quite the normal pronoun for the second person singular in ordinary conversation, the use of *"Thou"* and *"Thee"* was retained in the Revised Version; and, at that time, the use of *"You"* and *"Your"* in prayer would have provoked an enormous outcry. This is one of those changes that has really come about very suddenly in the last 40 years in conformity with what was said in chapter 2 about the increasing pace of change! I believe that modern translators of the Bible, should have accepted that the use of *"Thou"* and *"Thee"* in address to God was a centuries-old practice, a feature of our religious English, and therefore to be retained.

In the July 1979 issue of the Evangelical Times (from which I quote by kind permission) there were articles respectively on the use of *"Thou"* and of *"You."* The article on *"Thou"* by the Rev. Paul E. G. Cook was generally very good. Quoting the Oxford Dictionary definition of "archaic" as being "no longer in common use, though retained for special purposes," he makes the point that a word may be "archaic," but still relevant in a particular situation. He goes on:

> "Language 'retained for special purposes' may well be archaic, but its retention gives it the right to be regarded as modern language for the purpose for which it is used. Until the 1960s the use of *'Thou'* and *'Thee'* in

addressing God was more common than the use of *'You,'* even though the words had long ceased to be used in general conversation in the south of England. (He points out they are still used in the north!) They were still common usage for addressing God and still are. The usage is both archaic and modern.

"The question to be considered, therefore, is whether the use of *'Thou'* and *'Thee'* is still relevant to the relationship which ought to exist between the modern man and his God. We can hold on to traditions, even though they have ceased to be of any real contemporary value. But such is not the case here, since the tragedy of the modern man is that he seems to have lost all sense of the tremendous gulf which exists between the Creator and the creature....

"The whole problem of fallen man is that he is unaware of the disparity between himself and God. It is also the problem of the church today. A sense of awe and wonder in the presence of God has departed from the churches."

Mr. Cook ends his article with:

"Let us beware of too quickly abandoning the old paths in a desire to be modern. The quest for relevance can too easily lead to irrelevance. And many have gone that way. *'Thou'* is relevant; *'You'* is not."

But there is the important translation point to be considered also. It is often said that the AV is written in 16th/17th century English and while this is no doubt partly true in that everything is the product of its own age, yet it is not entirely true, especially as regards this question of the second person singular pronouns. The pronoun *"You"* started to be used instead of *"Thou"* towards the end of the 13th century, and this use extended in the following three centuries. But the translators of the AV did not conform to this rising usage, so that, when the AV appeared, it was not in some ways in the usage of the 17th century. Why did the AV translators not adopt the up-to-date English of their time? For one particular reason which many people have perhaps not realised — *accuracy of translation!* Whenever the Hebrew and Greek texts use the singular of the pronoun, so does the AV; and whenever those texts use the plural, so does the AV. In other words, the AV translators stuck closely to *the Biblical usage,* and translated the Word of God using a kind of Biblical style of English. The version was a faithful one above all else. The same cannot be said so completely for any other English Bible — in fact most are nowhere near that standard. There is a distinct loss of accuracy in translation if *"You"* is used for the singular as well as the plural: it becomes an ambiguous word. The AV informs us correctly on what was the proper original sense. Thus, in Luke 22. 31, 32, the Lord says to Peter "Satan hath desired to have *you,* that he may sift *you* as wheat," *"you"* here referring to Peter and the other disciples; "But I have prayed for *thee,* that *thy* faith fail not," *"thee"* and *"thy"* referring to Peter only. Such shades of meaning are completely lost when *"you"* is used throughout.

Some modern versions of the Bible have attempted to get round the point by modernising all the pronouns, except in speech addressed to God where *"Thou," "Thee,"* etc., are retained. As already noticed in chapter 3, the RSV and the NEB adopted this line. There are two strong objections to it. First, the Greek does not make such a distinction: it simply uses one pronoun for the singular and another for the plural (as does the AV). Secondly, these versions have generally treated the Lord Jesus Christ as man, and have therefore used *"you"* when He has been addressed, and *"thou"* when God the Father has been addressed. This distinction is disparaging of the person and glory of Christ, who is equal with the Father in power and glory. There are, of course, some cases where people addressed the Lord Jesus not realising that He was Divine, e.g. the woman of Samaria. It would be difficult to know how to treat these, even if *"Thou"* were being used in address to the Lord Jesus. It does not seem that this "halfway house" is at all satisfactory and it is interesting to see that both the RSV and the REB recently issued — the revision of the NEB — have abandoned it, and use *"You"* throughout. But the fact remains that the AV's usage is both correct as a translation, reverent and time-honoured, and children can certainly be educated to the use of *"Thou"* and *"Thee"* in worship if there is a mind so to educate them.

A fuller treatment of this whole subject, particularly from the point of view of grammar and language is given in Appendix B, which is an extract from the writings of Prof. O. T. Allis.

As a side-issue on this question, one dreads the thought of any "modernisation" of pronouns in our vast treasury of beautiful hymns in the English language. May we not be left to "despise our birthright" in this!

CHAPTER 7

THE NEW KING JAMES VERSION

I devote somewhat more detailed consideration to this version because it is closer to the AV than all the other modern versions, both in its textual basis and in its style of translation. Although the Hebrew text on which the Old Testament rests is somewhat different from that underlying the AV, the NKJV is the only modern version in which the New Testament is based on the traditional Greek text, in other words the same textual basis as in the AV. This gives a welcome indication that some modern scholars have adopted the traditional view of the Greek manuscripts, and have not been misled, as have so many, by the errors of Westcott and Hort in the last century. The version is to be commended in this basic aspect. One does, however, have a fear that at some future date the textual basis of the New Testament of the NKJV may be changed to the so-called Majority Text outlined at the end of Chapter 4. Both the NKJV and the Hodges/Farstad Majority Greek Text are published by Thomas Nelson Inc, of Nashville, Tennessee, and Dr. Farstad took a prominent part in both projects. We shall have to wait and see; but such a basis, though no doubt better supported by the majority of the extant Greek manuscripts, and more reliable than the Nestlé/UBS Greek text, would cause further confusion in the churches, being a further variant from the time-honoured and God-blessed text underlying the AV New Testament. Judging from the footnotes in the NKJV, such a change of textual basis would mean at least 300 detailed changes in the New Testament.

The preface to the NKJV pays generous tribute to the AV and goes on to state the aims of the present project, many of which are commendable, but there seems to be a shortfall in their accomplishment. In my view, the desire of the translators for a translation in good modern English has been carried too far. The style of English is good, and never descends to some of the colloquial phrases and paraphrases used in Bibles like the New English Bible, and Today's English Version. Much of it reads well and would probably be easier to understand for people who have not been brought up on the AV as many have. However, the NKJV has gone over to the use of *"You"* and *"Your"* throughout, dropping altogether the second person singular pronouns *"Thou," "Thee," "Thy"* and *"Thine,"* even in speech addressed to God — all in the interests of consistent modern English. This, to my mind, is its most serious defect, as discussed in the previous chapter. Some of the changes of detail seem to have been rather unnecessary — almost like change for change's sake — and some changes are not for the better, a few of which have doctrinal implications. To be fair, some parts are improvements, as to the words, compared with the AV, and might well be helpful to people who know little about the Bible, and have not been "brought up" on the AV. But there are parts that are certainly not so good as the AV. In some extensive reading of the NKJV, I have noticed a number of such passages, and I give below just half a dozen examples:

Deut. 32. 2.   AV   My doctrine shall drop as the rain.

                NKJV Let my teaching drop as the rain.

The NKJV version is not so positive and firm as the AV: it almost savours of human cooperation being required.

Prov. 16. 1.   AV   The preparations of the heart in
                     man, and the answer of the
                     tongue, is from the Lord.

               NKJV The preparations of the heart
                     belong to man. But the answer
                     of the tongue is from the Lord.

Dr. Gill mentions the kind of rendering given in the NKJV,
but both he and Matthew Henry support the AV rendering,
pointing out that in spiritual things we need the Holy Spirit
to influence our minds and hearts. The AV rendering is
consistent with Psalm 10. 17 and Philippians 2. 13.

Haggai 2. 7.   AV   And the desire of all nations
                     shall come.
               NKJV And they (i.e. the nations) shall
                     come to the Desire of All
                     Nations.

This text points to the coming Messiah, and the AV rendering
seems much to be preferred, and to be more fitting.

Romans 5. 4.   AV   And patience, experience; and
                     experience, hope.
               NKJV And perseverance, character; and
                     character, hope.

The AV rendering is plainer and preferable. In particular,
the Christian's hope is more derived from his *experience* of
God's dealings with him than from any features of his
character.

James 1. 16.   AV   Do not err.
               NKJV Do not be deceived.

"Being deceived" is only one aspect of "erring." The AV word is more comprehensive.

Rev. 19. 8.	AV	For the fine linen is the righteousness of saints.
	NKJV	For the fine linen represents the righteous acts of the saints.

The NKJV rendering has serious doctrinal implications. The original word in the Greek is in the plural i.e. righteousnesses. I understand that this is used in a distributive sense, that there is a complete righteousness — "the robe of righteousness" (Isaiah 61. 10) — for each and every believer. The AV translators were obviously mindful of the fact that to have translated the word literally as "righteousnesses" could, and would, have been misconstrued to give support for the teaching of salvation by works. But "righteous acts" as in the NKJV points even more directly to good works. We have much to be thankful for in the good rendering in the AV which points unequivocally to the righteousness of the Lord Jesus Christ being imputed to each and every believer.

There are other instances similar to the foregoing six that could be named. In addition, there are some words used in the NKJV to replace other quite well known words in the AV, and I consider them not to be so good and to have been unnecessary changes. For example:

NKJV		**AV**
End of the age	instead of	End of the world
Lawlessness	instead of	Iniquity
Mute	instead of	Dumb
Slaves	instead of	Servants
Sandals	instead of	Shoes
Bronze	instead of	Brass

"Thy shoes shall be iron and brass" has a much more familiar and supportive ring to it in the English-speaking world than "Your sandals shall be iron and bronze"! (Deuteronomy 33. 25).

Another feature of the NKJV is that the names of coins and other Roman things are retained, so that when Christ was asked about paying the Roman taxes, he said (in the NKJV) "Show me a denarius" instead of "Show me a penny," as in the AV. This of course is a more literal rendering because "denarius" was the actual name of this Roman coin — hence we used "d" for "pence" until decimal coinage was introduced. None the less the AV translation of "penny" is the simpler for an English child to understand!

On its general format, the NKJV is to be commended for continuing the AV practice of showing in italics words that have been supplied to clarify the translation. It also has paragraph headings which are generally good and helpful to the reader: but, here and there, the heading leaves something to be desired, e.g. "Do good to please God" over Matthew 6. 1-4 and "Free from indwelling sin" over Romans 8. 1-11. Romans 7 shows how much Paul felt the indwelling of sin, but the freedom of the 8th chapter is rather freedom from condemnation. The treatment of the Song of Solomon is very unusual, involving as it does a kind of dramatic presentation, as well as the paragraph headings. None of the headings, or names of speakers, refer to Christ, or His church as do the page headings and chapter headings (where provided) in the AV. One is fully aware that such headings are not part of the inspired Word of God, but all good Protestant commentators and ministers have always referred the Song of Solomon to Christ and His church and it seems a great loss to have this book left more or less as just an earthly song, and no reference at all to Him who really is "the chiefest among ten thousand'' and the ''altogether lovely.''

The NKJV also has footnotes. Some are simple cross-references, and some in the Old Testament give the literal Hebrew. In the New Testament there are many more footnotes, most being of a textual nature. The majority of these footnotes refer to the ''NU Text'' which is an abbreviation for the Nestlé-United Bible Societies Greek Text — the text which follows the principles of Westcott and Hort and on which most modern versions are based. These footnotes are no doubt of interest to scholars, but for the humble believer, they can be a trouble. Constantly to see ''NU text omits....'' or ''NU text reads....'' at the bottom of many pages can sow seeds of doubt, or perplexity, especially in younger minds, as to what is the true text. All these notes would have been better left out. A lesser number of footnotes in the New Testament refer to ''M-Text,'' which means ''Majority Text.'' This has already been discussed at the end of chapter 4. Suffice it to say here that the differences are not nearly as many or as weighty as those between the Traditional Text and the NU text. In short one feels that the NKJV footnotes constitute an undesirable feature of this version.

To sum up on the NKJV, it is a Bible in which you can read some pages and almost think you are reading the AV; but on other pages, the pronouns grate on one's ears, and one feels very unhappy about reading it. In some places, the translations may be slightly improved, but in others they are inferior. The difficulties of reading the AV, with its *"Thous"* and *"Thees,"* are frequently exaggerated; but if a person really has not the ability or the knowledge to read the AV — perhaps English is his second language — the NKJV is certainly the next-best to start with. It is more reliable than any other modern version. But for those who have been

New King James Version

"brought up" on the AV, or who can manage to read it, it is a retrograde step to go on to the NKJV. In the words of the "Brief History of the Trinitarian Bible Society" (page 119) the NKJV has "removed too much that was excellent in the older version."

Above all, we each need to remember that reading the Bible is not just a matter of intellect: "the natural man receiveth not the things of the Spirit of God... neither can he know them, because they are spiritually discerned" (1 Corinthians 2. 14). We do need the Holy Spirit of God to enlighten our understanding. Mercifully, He has promised the Holy Spirit "to them that ask" (Luke 11. 13), and may we be among such!

39

CHAPTER 8

THE MERITS OF THE AUTHORISED VERSION

Criticisms of the old-fashioned character of the language of the AV are often made, and are often exaggerated. It is true that some words have become archaic, and some have changed their meaning, since the AV was published. The TBS recognised this some years ago and published "A Bible Word List" to help with this problem. The Society is also considering ways of incorporating these up-to-date word meanings in the margin of an AV Bible so as to provide more ready means of assistance in reading the Scriptures. It is, further, often said that today's young people cannot cope with the second person singular pronouns *"Thou," "Thee,"* etc, and the old-fashioned verb endings such as "est" and "eth."
This may well be true, but it is more due to poor teaching of English, and of at least the rudiments of English grammar in our schools, than to anything else. There have been official reports on this deficiency in the last year or so. But children who can learn all about computers should be able to master the grammar of the second person singular! Otherwise what a lot of our heritage of literature they will be losing, not only in our incomparable version of the Bible, but also in Shakespeare's works, and the works of other famous writers. Our children need educating up to the AV, and not the AV being brought down to their level. Basically, the AV is in most parts simple to understand, especially perhaps in the Gospels, which have a high proportion of words of one syllable. Of course there are difficult passages to understand even naturally — parts of Ezekiel, and some of the other prophecies for example — but a new translation is not necessarily going to be much help. Often the ministry can be a help to younger folk on such passages. And, of course,

to understand the Scriptures spiritually, we are all utterly dependent on the light of the Holy Spirit. Many have proved that prayer for this light is the key to a real understanding of God's Word.

The language of the AV is majestic and beautiful, and so fitting to the divine message it has to convey. It is excellent for public reading, with its rhythmic cadences and stately words. It is certainly a literary master-piece, and a significant part of the nation's literary heritage, which we should do our best to conserve and pass on intact to our children. No less a personage than HRH the Prince of Wales had this aspect very much in mind when he spoke in December 1989 on the beauty of the language of Cranmer's Prayer Book and of the AV. It was refreshing to read the princely defence of the AV's language, and over the next week or so the supportive correspondence printed in The Daily Telegraph. Clearly there are many people still who do appreciate and cherish the language of the AV.

The Authorised Version is the best, the most trustworthy and the most accurate translation of the Holy Scriptures available in the English language. This is not to say that as a translation it is absolutely perfect, because it is not, and in some small details it could be improved. For example, in Acts 12. 4, the Greek word translated as "Easter" would be better translated as "passover." Neither is the AV as a translation "inspired": but to the extent that it faithfully reproduces in English the inspired words that God originally gave, it must partake of that same inspiration and divine authority, and one believes that faithful reproduction of those original words is its supreme quality. One evidence of this is the way that the blessing of Almighty God has singularly and greatly rested on the AV during four centuries (and also on versions in other languages based on much the same text, such as, for example, Luther's Bible in German, and the Statenvertaling in Dutch). Generations have lived on its truths, its precepts, and its promises, made spirit and life in their souls by the work of the Holy Spirit. Our forefathers died "in hope of eternal life," given them through this version of the Word of God.

Another evidence of its divine authority may at times be felt in our own hearts. Have we sometimes intended to do something, but God has sent His Word into our hearts with power, and we have realised it would not be His will to do it? So, contrary to all our natural inclinations, we have refrained, and sometimes afterwards proved how far God's wisdom transcended ours in the matter. Or have we sometimes determined *not* to do something, but God has applied some Scripture to our hearts, and the love of Christ has constrained us to do it, and we have proved blessing in following out that word? Or have there been words of Scripture fastened in our souls in convincing us of our sin, in reproving us, and then in granting us a hope in His mercy and then forgiveness of our sins? These are all demonstrations that our Bibles, as we have them in the AV, are blessed by God and have His authority stamped on them, and the generations of God's people over the years have proved these things, both in life and in death. No doubt many evangelicals in these days would claim to have received similar blessings or guidance from the NIV or some other modern version. My point, however, is to draw attention to the *very long history* of deep and widespread blessing that has attended the AV — a very positive indication of Divine approval of this faithful, trustworthy translation. Shall we then turn our backs on this pure version of the Holy Scriptures? Shall we give up this priceless heritage, both in its beautiful language and in its spirituality? God forbid! May He grant us grace to

"Hold fast the form of sound words," and to cleave to the old paths!

I conclude this chapter with some excellent remarks by Mr. J. C. Philpot M.A., a godly minister of the last century who was an outstanding editor of the "Gospel Standard" for over twenty years, on the merits of the Authorised Version as a translation. (See the February 1861 Gospel Standard, or Vol. II of J. C. Philpot's "Reviews.") He speaks of the simplicity of the truth itself and then the simplicity of the form under which the Holy Ghost has been pleased to reveal it. He then goes on to speak of "the grace and wisdom bestowed upon our translators to give us such a faithful and noble, clear and beautiful, yet simple and plain version. The blessing which has rested upon our English Bible in the thousands of souls who by it have been quickened and fed, liberated, sanctified, and saved, eternity alone can unfold. But much of this, under the blessing of God, has been due to the plain, simple, yet strong and expressive language which our translators were led to adopt. They were deeply penetrated with a reverence for the word of God, and, therefore, they felt themselves bound by a holy constraint to discharge their trust in the most faithful possible way. Under this divine constraint they were led to give us a translation unequalled for faithfulness to the original, and yet at the same time clothed in the purest and simplest English. How suitable is all this to the simplest understanding, and how in this way the most precious truths of God are brought down to the plainest and most uncultivated mind. No one can read, with an enlightened eye, the discourses of our blessed Lord without seeing what a divine simplicity ran through all His words; and our translators were favoured with heavenly wisdom to translate these words of the Lord into language as simple as that in which they first fell from His lips. What can exceed the simplicity and yet the beauty and blessedness of such declarations as these? — 'I am the bread of life:' 'I am the door;' 'I am the way, the truth, and the life:' 'I lay down My life for the sheep;' 'I am the vine:' 'God is love;' 'By grace ye are saved.' Even where the words are not strictly monosyllabic they are of the simplest kind, and as such are adapted to the capacity of every child of God, in whatever rank of life he may be. The blessedness of having not only such a Bible, but possessing such a translation of it can never be sufficiently valued. If the Scriptures had been written in a style of language which required a learned education and a cultivated mind to understand, how would they have been adapted to the poor of the flock? Or had our translators wrapped up the simple language of the original in high flown expressions, how it would have set the word of truth beyond the grasp of the poor of the flock! But now as soon as the blessed Spirit is pleased to communicate light and life to the soul, the Bible is open to the poorest man to read and to understand; and as the Lord the Spirit is pleased to raise up faith in his heart to believe the testimony, he can not only understand what he thus reads without the necessity of a worldly education, but, under the unction of His grace, can also feel its power and blessedness in his own soul.

"But apart from the blessing which it has been thus made to the family of God, our English Bible has been a national treasure. It has much interwoven itself with our national character, has set up a pure standard of religion and morality, and is daily influencing thousands of hearts to actions of kindness and benevolence, as well as exercising a widely-spread power in upholding good and condemning evil. This moral effect of the Bible, as distinct from its spiritual effect, is sometimes too much overlooked or undervalued, but is not less real and substantial. It is something akin to the effect produced on a congregation where truth is preached, or in a family where its heads are partakers of the grace of God. In a congregation, many are influenced by the truth who are not regenerated by it; in a family, the children are often affected by the parent's example and admonitions who are not reached by their grace. So, apart from its sanctifying influence on the vessels of mercy, the Bible has exercised an amazing amount of good on society at large; and in this sense has been made a great national blessing. But it is because the language of our Bible is such pure, simple, unaffected, idiomatic, intelligible English that it has become so thoroughly English a book, and has interwoven itself with our very laws and language.''

It is a matter for sorrow and regret that the moral and social effect described in this last paragraph has so greatly diminished in the 130 years since these remarks were written.

CHAPTER 9

IS A REVISION OF THE AUTHORISED VERSION NEEDED?

This is not a new question! Indeed, it was asked only 30 years or so after the AV was published in 1611! It was certainly a question that came into prominence, as we have seen, in the second half of the 19th century. In April 1857, Mr. J. C. Philpot M.A., mentioned at the close of the last chapter, gave his thoughts as follows on the question whether it would be desirable to have a new or revised edition of the Scriptures:

> "We fully admit that there are here and there passages of which the translation might be improved; as, for instance, 'love' for 'charity' throughout 1 Corinthians 13; but we deprecate any alteration as a measure that the smallest sprinkling of good would deluge us with a flood of evil. The following are our reasons:

> "1. Who are to undertake it? Into whose hands would the translation fall? What an opportunity for the enemies of truth to give us a mutilated false Bible! Of course they must be learned men, great critics, scholars and divines. But these are notoriously either tainted with popery or infidelity. Where are the men, learned, yet sound in Truth, not to say alive unto GOD, who possess the necessary qualifications for so important a work? and can erroneous men, DEAD IN TRESPASSES AND SINS, CARNAL, WORLDLY, UNGODLY persons, *spiritually translate* a book written by the BLESSED SPIRIT? We have not the slightest ground for hope that they would be godly men, such as we have reason to

believe translated the Scriptures into our present version.

"2. Again, it would unsettle the minds of thousands, as to which was the WORD OF GOD, the old translation or the new. What a door it would open for the workings of INFIDELITY, or the temptations of Satan! What a gloom too, it would cast over the minds of many of God's saints, to have those passages which had been applied to their souls translated in a different way, and how it would seem to shake all their experience of the power and preciousness of GOD'S WORD!

"3. But besides all this, there would be two Bibles spread throughout all the land, the old and the new, and what confusion would this create in almost every place! At present, all sects and denominations agree in acknowledging our present version as to the standard of appeal. Nothing settles disputes so soon as when the contending parties have confidence in the same umpire and are willing to abide by his decision. But this judge of all dispute, this umpire of all controversy would cease to be the looser of strife if present acknowledged authority were put an end to by a rival.

"4. If the new translation were once to begin, where would it end? It is good to let well alone, as it is easier to mar than to mend. The Socinianising Neologian would blot out 'GOD' in 1 Timothy 3. 16, and strike out 1 John 5. 7, as an interpolation. The Puseyite* would mend it to suit his Tractarian views. He would

---

* Followers of E. B. Pusey and forerunners of Anglo-Catholics.

47

read 'priest' where we now read 'elder,' and put 'penance' in place of repentance. Once set up a notice: 'The old Bible to be mended' and there would be plenty of workmen, who, trying to mend the cover, would pull the pages to pieces. The Arminians would soften down the words 'Election' and 'Predestination' into some term less displeasing to Pharisaic ears. 'Righteousness' would be turned into 'Justice' and 'Reprobate' into 'Undiscerning.' All our good Bible terms would be so mutilated that they would cease to convey the Spirit's meaning and instead of the noble simplicity, faithfulness and truth of our present version, we should have a Bible that nobody would accept as the WORD OF GOD, to which none could safely appeal, and on which none implicitly rely.

"5. Instead of our good old Saxon Bible, simple and solid, with few words obsolete, and alike majestic and beautiful, we should have a modern English translation in pert and flippant language of the day. Besides its authority as the WORD OF GOD, our present version is the great English Classic — generally accepted as the standard of the English language. The great classics of a language cannot be modernised. What an outcry there would be against modernising Shakespeare, or making Hooker, Bacon or Milton, talk the English of the newspapers or of the House of Commons.

"6. The present English Bible (Authorised Version) has been blessed to thousands of the saints of GOD; and not only so, it has become part of our national inheritance which we have received unimpaired from our fathers, and are bound to hand down unimpaired to our children. It is we believe, the grand bulwark of Protestantism; the safeguard of the gospel, and the treasure of the Church; and we should be traitors in every sense of the word if we consented to give it up to be rifled by the sacrilegious hands of the Puseyites, concealed papists, German Neologians, infidel divines, Arminians, Socinians and the whole tribe of enemies of GOD and godliness.''

Mr. Philpot died in 1869, and within 15 years of his death, much of what he foresaw had been fulfilled. The Revised Version had appeared, and what had started as an exercise in revising the AV had turned into a much deeper revision, based on a different and less reliable underlying text. What would he have said about all the versions we have nowadays, and all the confusion which, as he foresaw, would thereby be sown among the Churches! What he said in 1857 still applies today, and we certainly have even less conservative evangelical scholars to do a new translation than there were in his day. On the other hand, another 130 years having elapsed, the language of the AV is even more out-of-date, and this is the point usually made in favour of a new translation, more especially for the benefit of the younger generation.

Let us hear what another eminent minister of our own day and from a different background had to say on this subject. The late Dr. Martyn Lloyd-Jones, addressed a rally at the Royal Albert Hall in 1961, and the following is an extract from what he said on that occasion in reference to the AV:

"I suppose that the most popular of all the proposals at the present moment is to have a new translation of the Bible.... The argument is that people are not reading the Bible any longer because they do not understand its language — particularly the archaic terms — what does your modern man... know about justification, sanctification, and all these Biblical terms? And so we are told the one thing that is necessary is to have a translation that Tom, Dick and Harry will understand, and I began to feel about six months ago that we had almost reached the stage in which the Authorised Version was being dismissed, to be thrown into the limbo of things forgotten, no longer of any value. Need I apologise for saying a word in favour of the Authorised Version in this gathering?....

"It is a basic proposition laid down by the Protestant Reformers, that we must have a Bible 'understanded of the people.' That is common sense... we must never be obscurantists. We must never approach the Bible in a mere antiquarian spirit... but it does seem to me that there is a very grave danger incipient in so much of the argument that is being presented today for these new translations. There is a danger, I say, of our surrendering something that is vital and essential....

"Take this argument that the modern man does not understand such terms as justification, sanctification and so on. I want to ask a question. When did the ordinary man ever understand those terms?.... Did the colliers to whom John Wesley and George Whitefield preached in the 18th century understand? They had not even been to a day school... they could not read, they could not write. Yet these were the terms that were used. This was the version that was used — the Authorised Version. The common people have never understood these terms.... We are concerned here with something that is spiritual; something which does not belong to this world at all; which, as the Apostle Paul reminds us, the princes of this world do not know. Human wisdom is of no value here — it is a spiritual truth. This is truth about God primarily, and because of that it is a mystery....

''Yet we are told — it must be put in such simple terms and language that anybody taking it up and reading it is going to understand all about it. My friends, this is sheer nonsense. What we must do is to educate the masses of the people up to the Bible, not bring the Bible down to their level. One of the greatest troubles today is that everything is being brought down to the same level, everything is cheapened. The common man is made the standard of authority; he decides everything, and everything has to be brought down to him....

''Are we to do that with the Word of God? I say No! What has happened in the past has been this — ignorant, illiterate people, in this country and in foreign countries, coming into salvation have been educated up to the Book and have begun to understand it, to glory in it, and to praise God for it, and I say that we need to do the same at this present time. What we need is therefore, not to replace the Authorised Version... we need rather to reach and train people up to the standard and the language, the dignity and the glory of the old Authorised Version.''

What a lot of truth there is in what Dr. Lloyd-Jones said! But let us now take a glance at the practical side. At present, and with the recent take-over of Eyre and Spottiswoode's publishing by Cambridge University Press, there are only three publishers in this country who are legally able to print the AV, namely, the Cambridge University Press, the Oxford University Press and Messrs Collins of Glasgow. If it were desired to make a *revision* of the AV (as distinct from a new translation), say on a "minimum-change" basis, the revision would have to be done through these firms, and with their agreement. By a "minimum change" I mean the replacement of archaic words and words that have changed their meaning, and also of a few expressions no longer current in polite usage, but not extending (in my judgment) to the replacement of *"Thou,"* *"Thee,"* etc. But doubtless there would be pressure, whether from the publishers or from others concerned with the project, to go further and switch to the more modern *"You,"* *"Your,"* etc., and perhaps to make some other revisions. There is thus a very real risk that if once the door were opened to a very modest up-dating of the AV, the whole matter might go further than many of us would wish, and thus, in Mr. Philpot's words, "the smallest sprinkling of good would deluge us with a flood of evil." It could even be that the AV, as we now know it, would more or less disappear.

If a separate new translation were put forward, the position would be different, and the AV would still be available so long as there was a reasonable level of demand for it. It may be that, in the course of time, and as the generations who have been brought up on the AV with its "old-fashioned" pronouns move off this earthly scene, the pressure for a completely new translation on a sound textual basis and in good modern English will increase and have to be met. If so, one devoutly hopes that the textual basis will be kept the same as that underlying the AV, and that the translation will be done in the noblest and most appropriate English. We all have to realise that, in God's ordering of things, language — like all other things in this world — does change, and sometimes there are particular eras in a nation's history when it changes fast. But, as things are at present, we would be thankful that the AV was written in an English that was "biblical" (as pointed out earlier), and that it was also as "timeless" as it was possible to write. Furthermore, in the last analysis, faithfulness and purity of translation are more important than modern language. As we enter the 1990s, with all the changes we have seen in the last 50 years, and as we look around at all the Bible versions currently available, we can only say, as the Lord Jesus said (Luke 5. 39): "No man also having drunk old wine straightway desireth new: for he saith, THE OLD IS BETTER."

APPENDIX A

BIBLIOGRAPHY

Note — "TBSL" = TBS Leaflet, obtainable from The Trinitarian Bible Society, 217 Kingston Road, London, SW19 3NN, at a small charge.

GENERAL

The Divine Inspiration of the Holy Scripture	TBSL 66
What is wrong with the modern versions?	TBSL 41
Holding fast the faithful Word	TBSL 56

Which Bible?   Dr. D. O. Fuller

True or False?   Dr. D. O. Fuller
— A Sequel to Which Bible?
Each of these two books provides a very useful symposium on the whole subject. Very faithful to the Received Text.

Published by Grand Rapids International Publications, Grand Rapids, Michigan 49501, U.S.A. Obtainable in U.K. from Tabernacle Book Shop, Elephant & Castle, London. SE1 6SD.

The King James Version Defended
Dr. E. F. Hills
(This book is obtainable from Penfold Book and Bible House, P.O. Box 26 Bicester, Oxon. OX6 8PB.)

Believing Bible Study   Dr. E. F. Hills
These two books cover much the same ground but in different ways.
Very faithful to the Received Text.

Published by The Christian Research Press, P.O. Box 2013, Des Moines, Iowa, 50310, U.S.A.

The Identity of the New Testament Text
Dr. W. N. Pickering
A very technical, scholarly book, defending well the Traditional Text in general but adumbrating a Majority Text position in due course.

Published by Thomas Nelson Inc., Nashville, Tennessee, U.S.A.

54

Appendix A

The Future of the Bible   Dr. Jakob van Bruggen
An excellent book in many ways, defending the
Traditional Text, but leaning ultimately to a
Majority Text position.

Published by
Thomas Nelson Inc.,
Nashville,
Tennessee, U.S.A.

The Majority Text — Essays and Reviews
Edited by Theodore P. Letis
A scholarly symposium giving various aspects of
the Majority Text question and defending the
Received Text.

Published by
Institute for
Textual Studies,
Grand Rapids,
Michigan, U.S.A.

CHAPTER 3 — **The main English versions**

The AV	See under Chapters 8 and 9 below	
The RSV	The Divine Original (Deficiencies in RSV)	TBSL 13
	Rome and the RSV	TBSL 5
The NEB	Critical review of the NEB	TBSL 12
The NASV	A brief review	TBSL 46
Today's English Version (The Good News Bible)		TBSL 6
	A review	
The New Jerusalem Bible	A review	TBSL 73
The Living Bible	A brief review	TBSL 18
The NIV	A brief review	TBS Quarterly Record, Jan.-March 1974
	Another look	TBSL 19A
	Should we trust the NIV?	Leaflet from Focus Christian Ministries Trust, 6 Orchard Road, Lewes, E. Sussex. BN7 2HB
	Accuracy of Translation and the NIV. Robert Martin A very useful appraisal	Banner of Truth Trust (also obtainable from Tabernacle Bookshop as above)

Appendix A

The NKJV	See under Chapter 7 below	
The REB	Review	TBS Quarterly Record Oct.-Dec. 1989
Jehovah's Witnesses Versions		TBSL 67

CHAPTER 4 — **The Hebrew & Greek Texts**

The books quoted under the GENERAL Section of this
Bibliography

| The New Testament manuscripts | TBS Quarterly Record Jan.-March 1990 |

CHAPTER 5 — **Thoughts on Translations**

The books quoted under the GENERAL Section of this
Bibliography

| Accuracy of Translation and the NIV. Robert Martin Includes an excellent treatment of "Dynamic Equivalence" | Banner of Truth Trust (also obtainable from Tabernacle Bookshop, as above) |

CHAPTER 6 — **"Thou" or "You"**

| Article "Unto thee will I pray" | TBS Quarterly Record Jan.-March 1980 |

CHAPTER 7 — **The NKJV**

New Testament	Review	TBS Quarterly Record Apr.-June 1980
Complete Bible	Review	TBSL 71
Remarks on the NKJV — Booklet by D. K. Madden A good 24 pages detailed critique of the NKJV		35 Regent Street, Sandy Bay, Tasmania, 7005, Australia.

Appendix A

CHAPTERS 8 and 9 — **The Authorised Version**

The men behind the KJV. — Gustavus S. Paine
An interesting book about the 1604-11 translators
and how their work was accomplished

Published by
Baker Book House,
Grand Rapids,
Michigan, U.S.A.
(also obtainable
from Tabernacle
Bookshop as above)

The Learned Men (the translators)   TBSL 25
How we got our Bible   TBSL 15
The excellence of the Authorised Version   TBSL 24
Plain reasons why we keep to the AV   TBSL 63
The Translators' Preface — "The Translators to the   Obtainable from
Reader."   Focus
Written by Dr. Miles Smith   Christian Ministries
                                           Trust, as above.

APPENDIX B

Is a Pronominal Revision of the Authorised Version Desirable?

by Oswald T. Allis

THE FARTHER TRANSLATORS depart from the style of the document they are translating, the more complicated does their problem become, the greater will be the variety in the translations proposed, and the greater will be the danger of the translation becoming an interpretation. Dr. Burrows lays down what we believe to be the true governing principle for all accurate translating, when he says, ''The translator can only follow his text, leaving it for the commentator to explain.'' Many of the difficulties in which revisers have become involved are the direct result of their failure to observe this fundamental rule. An especially important example of this, because of its doctrinal implications, is their rendering of the second person singular where it occurs in the Greek text.

THE FORMS "THOU," "THY," "THINE"

It is a well-known fact that in contemporary English the forms *''thou,'' ''thy,'' ''thine''* have almost disappeared from secular use. They are largely restricted to the language of religious devotion, in which they are constantly employed, and which is largely formed by and owes its peculiarities to the Authorised Version. Consequently, it is often asserted or assumed that the usage of AV represents the speech of 300 years ago, and that now, three centuries later, it should be changed to accord with contemporary usage.

But this is not at all a correct statement of the problem. The important fact is this. The usage of AV is *not* the ordinary usage of the early 17th century: it is the Biblical usage based on the style of the Hebrew and the Greek Scriptures. The second part of this statement needs no proof and will be challenged by no one. It is undeniable that where the Hebrew and Greek use the singular of the pronoun the AV regularly uses the singular, and where they use the plural it uses the plural. Even in Deuteronomy where in his addresses, and apparently for rhetorical and pedagogical effect, Moses often changes suddenly and seemingly arbitrarily from singular to plural or from plural to singular, AV reproduces the style of the text with fidelity. That is to say, the usage of the AV is strictly Biblical.

58

Appendix B

The first part of the above statement is not quite so easy to prove, but there is abundant evidence to support it. According to the late Professor Lounsbury of Yale, the substitution of the plural for the singular in addressing an individual "made its appearance in the English language toward the close of the 13th century.... In the 14th and 15th centuries the use of the plural steadily increased, and in the 16th century it became the standard form of polite conversation.... For some two centuries it may be said that in a general way they (the *'thou'* and *'thee'*) were employed to denote affection or inferiority or contempt."

Examples of these three uses are to be found in Shakespeare, for example, in *Henry V.* Lounsbury was especially concerned to illustrate the last of the three, contempt. If the correctness of Lounsbury's statement is admitted it is quite obvious that the AV did not attempt to make the usage of the Hebrew and Greek conform to the usage of the Elizabethan or early Jacobean period. It simply followed the Biblical usage, despite the fact that for some 300 years the trend had been increasingly away from it. Needless to say, the two earlier revisions of the AV — the English Revised Version of 1881 and the American Revised Version of 1901 — followed the AV in this regard, despite the fact that the ordinary usage in the years 1880-1900 was much the same as it is today.

The following words of A. T. Robertson are worthy of careful pondering in this connection: "No one today speaks the English of the King James Version, or ever did for that matter, for though, like Shakespeare, it is the pure Anglo-Saxon, yet unlike Shakespeare it reproduces to a remarkable extent the spirit and language of the Bible" (*A Grammar of the Greek NT,* page 56). This is its great claim to distinction, the reason it has endeared itself to multitudes of English-speaking people for more than three centuries: it *reproduces to a remarkable extent the spirit and language of the Bible.*

LANGUAGE ADDRESSED TO THE LORD JESUS

There is another very important consideration. If the second person singular is to be used only "in language addressed to God," what is to be done in the case of language addressed to Jesus the Christ? Is *"thou"* to be used regularly, because He is God, whether so regarded by the speaker or not? Is *"you"* to be used regularly, because He was, or, it is assumed, was regarded by the speaker as man? Or, is the translator to exegete each passage and decide dogmatically which of these pronouns is to be used in a given case? For example, in Matthew 16. 16, the words of Peter's confession at Caesarea Philippi are rendered in the Revised Standard Version (RSV), "You are the Christ, the Son of the living God." Here, in reply to a direct question as to what Jesus' apostles and immediate followers held Him to be, Peter affirms that He is the Messiah of Old Testament prophecy, that He is the Son of the living God. Yet several modern versions use *"you"* here instead of *"thou"* (cf. also Matthew 14. 33; 20. 21).

We turn to Mark 1. 11 and Luke 3. 22 and there, according to the RSV, the living God addresses His "Son" with *"Thou."* Does this affirm Jesus' Deity, or does it not? In Acts 1. 24 the "Lord" is addressed with *"thou"* (RSV). Does this mean that God is addressed, or that Jesus is addressed as *God?* Since Jesus chose His twelve apostles while He was on earth, it would be natural to suppose that this prayer for guidance in the choice of a successor to Judas would be addressed to Him in heaven (cf. Acts 9. 13 with 4. 24-27). Is such the intent of the revisers? We note in this connection that the risen but not yet ascended Christ is addressed as *"you"* in Acts 1. 6 (RSV). Finally, we turn to Hebrews where, in the first chapter, the unique dignity of this Son of the living God is elaborately proved by six or seven quotations from the Old Testament. In four of these the pronoun of the second singular is used. RSV renders it here by *"thou"* or *"thy."*

It is important to remember that the retention of the distinction between the singular and the plural is sometimes quite essential to accuracy of rendering. *"You,"* as both singular and plural, is at times confusing in English, as in French and German, and requires explanation if used for both, as for instance in Luke 22. 31f., where by the use of *"you,"* the distinction between the apostles (or disciples) and "thee" (Peter) disappears.

In Acts 13. 47 Paul introduces a quotation from the Old Testament with the words, "For so hath the Lord commanded us, saying." Then follow the familiar words from Isaiah 49. 6 which a modern translation renders "I have set you to be a light for the Gentiles that you may bring salvation to the uttermost parts of the earth." *"You"* suggests Paul and Barnabas and by implication every ambassador of Christ. Hence, it is important to note that in the Hebrew and the Greek the pronoun is not plural but singular, and the *"thou"* suggests an individual primarily, the Messiah.

THE REAL ISSUE

The real issue is whether or not we are prepared to give up the use of the singular of the pronoun entirely, and to this there are two main objections. The first is that it gives up the attempt to retain in English a distinction which is clearly drawn in Hebrew and in Greek. The second is that it means that *"thou"* and *"thee"* and *"thy"* are to pass completely out of 20th century English. The singular form of the pronoun is not even to be tolerated in the language of devotion and worship. It is to disappear from the Lord's Prayer and give place to "Your name be revered," "Your kingdom come"! Scores of our most familiar and best-loved hymns will then have to be discarded or more or less drastically edited. And the liturgies of the liturgical churches (e.g. the *Te Deum*) will need a thorough overhauling, if such a radical change is to be carried through. It is only in very recent days that Christian people have raised objections to the former language of devotion and worship. When the present century began people did not raise objections to what we may call a Scriptural and Biblical style as the language of devotion and worship. They liked it. They did not want the Bible to read just like any other book, to have the up-to-the-minute style of the daily newspaper. They loved its quaint, if you wish to call it that, its distinctive, its Biblical way of putting things. And we believe that the great majority of them do so today.

Why should the *"thou"* which is reserved for Deity be used in quotations from the Old Testament which speak of the Messiah, if it is not to be used in a New Testament passage which expressly affirms the Messiahship of Jesus as the Son of the living God? Is the Old Testament in the RSV to have a more archaic style than the New Testament? Hardly, for *"you"* appears in some quotations from it. If "Thou art My Son, today I have begotten Thee," which is a quotation from a Psalm, is a proper rendering for Hebrews 1. 5 in the RSV, why should we read, "You are the Christ, the Son of the living God" in Matthew 16. 16? To prove that the rendering in RSV is arbitrary, inconsistent and highly interpretive, it is sufficient to compare Matthew 20. 21 with Matthew 25. 37-45.